ON THE HUNT

WILD HOG HUNTING

BY ROXANNE TROUP

EPIC

BELLWETHER MEDIA • MINNEAPOLIS, MN

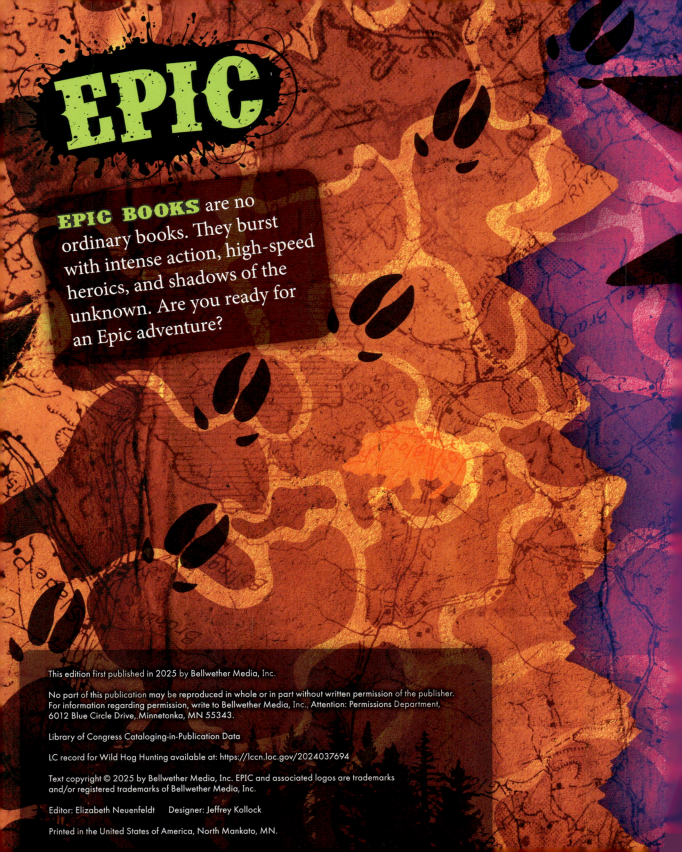

EPIC

EPIC BOOKS are no ordinary books. They burst with intense action, high-speed heroics, and shadows of the unknown. Are you ready for an Epic adventure?

This edition first published in 2025 by Bellwether Media, Inc.

No part of this publication may be reproduced in whole or in part without written permission of the publisher. For information regarding permission, write to Bellwether Media, Inc., Attention: Permissions Department, 6012 Blue Circle Drive, Minnetonka, MN 55343.

Library of Congress Cataloging-in-Publication Data

LC record for Wild Hog Hunting available at: https://lccn.loc.gov/2024037694

Text copyright © 2025 by Bellwether Media, Inc. EPIC and associated logos are trademarks and/or registered trademarks of Bellwether Media, Inc.

Editor: Elizabeth Neuenfeldt   Designer: Jeffrey Kollock

Printed in the United States of America, North Mankato, MN.

TABLE OF CONTENTS

TRACKING A HOG	4
WHAT IS WILD HOG HUNTING?	6
NEEDED GEAR	12
SAFETY FIRST	16
GLOSSARY	22
TO LEARN MORE	23
INDEX	24

TRACKING A HOG

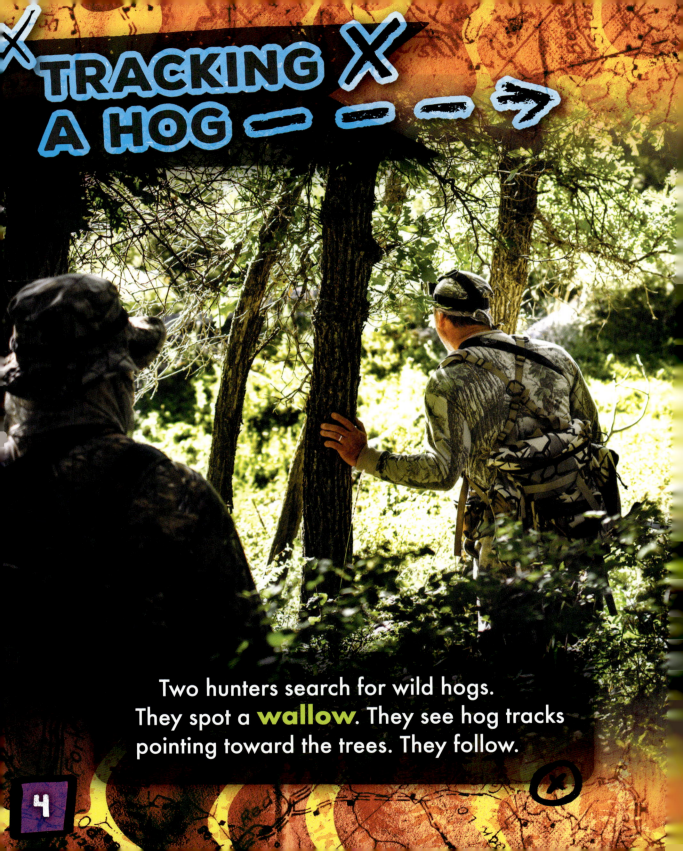

Two hunters search for wild hogs. They spot a **wallow**. They see hog tracks pointing toward the trees. They follow.

4

Suddenly, the hunters hear a grunt. It is a hog! But it is too fast. It gets away!

wallow

WHAT IS WILD HOG HUNTING?

Wild hogs are an **invasive species**. They have few **predators**. Hogs destroy land. They are dangerous. They can carry diseases.

WILD HOG RANGE

= range

United States

Some states trap wild hogs to get rid of them. Others allow people to hunt them.

Some states let people hunt wild hogs all year. Others limit hunting to the fall.

In some states, people can hunt with **bait**. In others, hunters **stalk** hogs.

FAVORITE HUNTING SPOT

NUECES RIVER BASIN, TEXAS

Texas

☑ Large wild hog population

☑ Year-round hunting

bait

stalking

FAR FROM HOME

Wild hogs are from Southeast Asia. People brought them to the Americas for food. Today, wild hogs are mostly found across the southern United States.

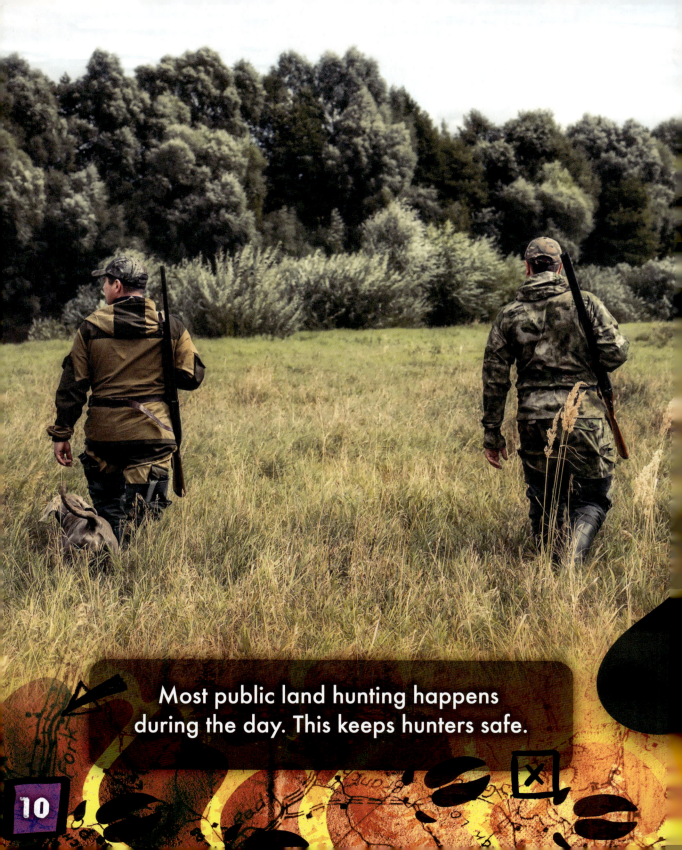

Most public land hunting happens during the day. This keeps hunters safe.

But hogs are most active at night. A few states allow night hunts on public land.

NEEDED GEAR

trail camera

Some people hunt wild hogs with trained dogs. Others depend on **trail cameras** and bait.

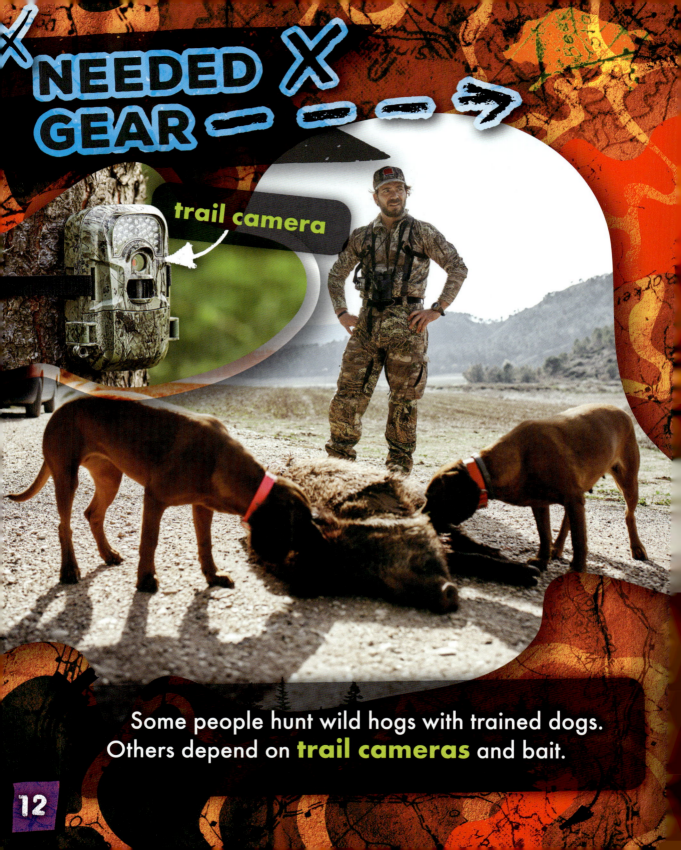

HUNTING GEAR

rifle with ammo

bait

trail camera

gloves

ammo

Hogs have a good sense of smell and a tough **hide**. Hunters cannot get too close. They need a hunting rifle with heavy **ammo**.

13

guide

Many hunters hire local guides. These people know where to find wild hogs. They know hunting rules. They may also have access to **private land**.

IN THE SPOTLIGHT

Hunting at night requires special gear. People use red and green spotlights or special rifles to see in the dark.

Many guides offer to rent gear to hunters.

SAFETY FIRST ---->

tusks

Wild hogs can be dangerous. They have sharp **tusks**. They carry diseases. If cornered, they may attack.

Hunters must stay alert. They should plan **escape routes**. They should wear gloves when handling wild hog bodies.

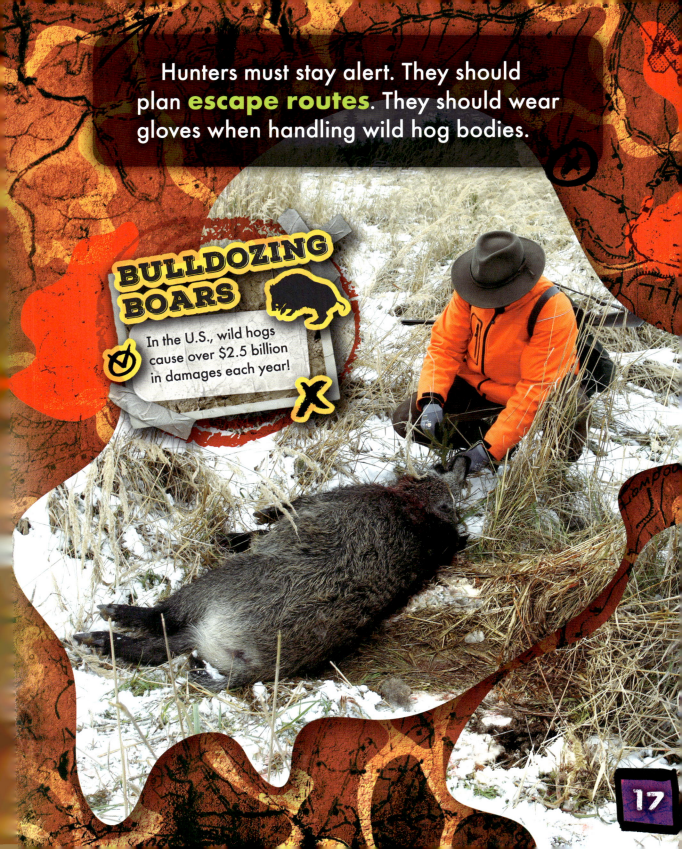

BULLDOZING BOARS

In the U.S., wild hogs cause over $2.5 billion in damages each year!

ethical shot placement

People should practice shooting before hunting. Hunters need to make **ethical shots**.

Wild hogs are also hard to shoot.
They run when scared and are hard to track.

Each state has different rules for hunting wild hogs. Hunters must follow the rules in their state. They may need to get a **license**.

Following the rules keeps everyone safe. It protects the land, too!

GLOSSARY

ammo—short for ammunition; ammo is often bullets.

bait—food left to attract an animal

escape routes—paths to exit dangerous situations

ethical shots—clean shots that reduce pain and suffering to animals

hide—animal skin

invasive species—a species not originally from a region that causes harm to its new region

license—a document that gives hunters legal permission to harvest a certain type of animal

predators—animals that hunt other animals for food

private land—land not owned by the government

stalk—to follow quietly and carefully

trail cameras—outdoor video cameras used to spot wildlife

tusks—long, pointed teeth

wallow—a muddy area where wild hogs roll around

TO LEARN MORE

AT THE LIBRARY

Clarke, Ginjer L. *Animal Invaders: Creatures Causing Trouble*. New York, N.Y.: Penguin Random House, 2023.

Sommer, Nathan. *American Alligator vs. Wild Boar*. Minneapolis, Minn.: Bellwether Media, 2023.

Wilson, Libby. *Wild Boars*. Mendota Heights, Minn.: North Star Editions, 2023.

ON THE WEB

Factsurfer.com gives you a safe, fun way to find more information.

1. Go to www.factsurfer.com.

2. Enter "wild hog hunting" into the search box and click 🔍.

3. Select your book cover to see a list of related content.

INDEX

Americas, 9
ammo, 13
bait, 8, 9, 12
damages, 17
day, 10
dogs, 12
escape routes, 17
ethical shots, 18
fall, 8
favorite hunting spot, 8
gloves, 17
guides, 14, 15
hide, 13
hunters, 4, 5, 8, 10, 13, 14, 15, 17, 18, 20
hunting gear, 13, 15
invasive species, 6

license, 20
night, 11, 15
predators, 6
private land, 14
public land, 10, 11
range, 7
rifle, 13, 15
rules, 14, 20
safety, 10, 16, 17, 20
Southeast Asia, 9
stalk, 8, 9
states, 7, 8, 11, 20
trail cameras, 12
trap, 7
tusks, 16
United States, 9
wallow, 4, 5

The images in this book are reproduced through the **courtesy of:** Eric Isselee, cover, p. 3; Cavan Images/ Alamy, pp. 4, 13; Kyslynskahal, pp. 5, 6, 7 (range); David_Hamburg, p. 5 (wallow); The Jungle Explorer, p. 7; PRESSLAB, p. 9; photowind, p. 9 (bait); AndreyUG, p. 10; Esteban Sanchez, p. 11; ADDICTIVE STOCK CREATIVES/ Alamy, p. 12; Krasula, pp. 12 (trail camera), 13 (trail cameras); David Schliepp, p. 13 (ammo); SolidMaks, p. 13 (rifle); ludovikus, p. 13 (bait); sweet marshmallow, p. 13 (gloves); Wayne Huges/ Alamy, p. 14; EXTREME-PHOTOGRAPHER/ Getty Images, p. 15; WildMedia, p. 16 (main, tusks); imageBroker.com GmbH & Co. KG/ Alamy, p. 17; PavelRodimov, p. 18; Geza Farkas, p. 19; Bill Gozansky/ Alamy, p. 20; Roman Kosolapov, p. 21; samodelkin8, p. 23.